Rembrandt

te looks a
tle gloomy.

Maybe he should use more colors!

BY DARICE BAILER • ILLUSTRATED BY J.T. MORROW

Published by The Child's World®
1980 Lookout Drive • Mankato, MN 56003-1705
800-599-READ • www.childsworld.com

Acknowledgments
The Child's World®: Mary Berendes, Publishing Director
Red Line Editorial: Editorial direction and production
The Design Lab: Design

Photographs ©: Rembrandt van Rijn, cover, 1, 5, 7, 8, 10–11, 12, 13, 14, 17, 18, 19, 21

ISBN 9781626873544
LCCN 2014930693

Printed in the United States of America
Mankato, MN
July, 2014
PA02223

ABOUT THE AUTHOR

Darice Bailer is the author of many books for young readers. She has won a Parents' Choice Gold Award and a Parents' Choice Approved Seal for her work.

ABOUT THE ILLUSTRATOR

J.T. Morrow has worked as a freelance illustrator for more than 25 years and has won several awards. His work has appeared in advertisements, on packaging, in magazines, and in books. He lives near San Francisco, California, with his wife and daughter.

CONTENTS

CHAPTER 1

A Great Painter 4

CHAPTER 2

Growing Up in Holland 6

CHAPTER 3

On Top of the World. 10

CHAPTER 4

The Night Watch 16

Glossary 22

To Learn More 23

Index 24

CHAPTER 1
A Great Painter

Rembrandt is one of the most famous painters of all time. He lived in Holland during the 1600s. He introduced new kinds of painting. He is known for how he painted light and dark. Rembrandt is so famous that people know him by his first name. His paintings sell for millions of dollars.

Rembrandt lived before there were cameras and photographs. If parents wanted a picture of their child, they needed one painted. Rembrandt's pictures were realistic, like photos. They were very expressive. He used a paintbrush to help us see into a girl's eyes. Was the child he painted happy? Or was she dreaming of playing outside? It's hard to tell what people are thinking by looking at them. But Rembrandt tried to show us with the tip of his brush and tiny flecks of paint.

Some of Rembrandt's most famous works are portraits of himself. His paintings, **etchings**, and drawings are like photographs of his life.

REMBRANDT'S ETCHINGS
Rembrandt used a sharp etching needle. He carved his design on a thin copper plate. Next he covered the plate with ink. He wiped off all the ink except the ink in the grooved design. Then he turned the plate over onto a sheet of paper. Finally he rolled the paper through a press. The press stamped his image.

He looks a little gloomy.

Maybe he should use more colors!

One of Rembrandt's **self-portraits** was given to a king of England. Today, Rembrandt's paintings hang in famous museums. They are loved and admired by people around the world.

Rembrandt's use of light and dark is dramatic.

CHAPTER 2

Growing Up in Holland

Rembrandt was born in Holland on July 15, 1606. He grew up in the city of Leiden. It was Holland's second-biggest city, after Amsterdam. Rembrandt's father owned a large windmill. Farmers brought him bags of barley grains. The four wooden sails turned and helped grind up the barley inside.

Rembrandt started school when he was seven. He also took drawing lessons. Rembrandt discovered that he liked painting and drawing. In the 1600s, teenage boys often quit school to learn a **trade** or craft. One of Rembrandt's older brothers was a shoemaker. Another was a baker. Rembrandt wanted to paint.

A child like Rembrandt could work for a painter. Parents paid the painter to teach their child. When Rembrandt was 15, he became an **apprentice** to a painter in town. Inside the painter's workshop, Rembrandt tacked **canvas** on wood. He mixed paint. He watched the artist work. And he cleaned up brushes and paint at the end of each day.

Rembrandt worked for the painter for several years. He learned everything he could from that artist. His father thought a famous painter in Amsterdam could teach his

son more. The artist's name was Pieter Lastman. Lastman painted bright, colorful pictures. Some of his paintings showed events in history. Others illustrated stories from the Bible. Rembrandt moved to Amsterdam to study with Lastman around 1624. By 1625, Rembrandt moved back to Leiden. There he opened his own **studio**.

REMBRANDT'S FULL NAME

Rembrandt's full name was Rembrandt Harmenszoon van Rijn. Van Rijn means "from the Rhine River" in Dutch. Harmenszoon means son of Harmen. Harmen was Rembrandt's father's name.

Rembrandt painted this self-portrait in 1629 when he was about 23 years old.

Lastman taught Rembrandt how to show what a person was feeling with paint. Rembrandt practiced it in a painting in 1626. His painting is called *Tobit and Anna with the Kid*. It's a story from the Bible. A couple named Tobit and Anna were very poor. Tobit heard a kid, or young goat, bleating and thought Anna stole it. But he was wrong because the goat was a gift. On canvas, Rembrandt showed how sorry Tobit was. Tobit clasped his hands and begged Anna for forgiveness.

The figures of Tobit and Anna are full of emotion.

In Leiden, Rembrandt often drew people he knew. He painted a picture of his mother and sister. He drew himself, too. One day he sketched himself laughing. Another time Rembrandt painted himself with his hair standing up. He didn't comb his curly hair very neatly.

A secretary for a Dutch prince saw one of Rembrandt's paintings. The secretary's name was Constantijn Huygens. Huygens couldn't believe how talented Rembrandt was. How could a young miller's son show so much emotion with a paintbrush? The secretary believed that the painting was a **masterpiece**.

CHAPTER 3

On Top of the World

Meeting the prince's secretary was lucky for Rembrandt. Huygens was so impressed that he asked Rembrandt to paint for the prince. Huygens asked Rembrandt to paint two pictures first. Both were about Jesus, the central figure in the Christian religion. Rembrandt mixed up his paint and went to work.

In the meantime, Rembrandt was becoming famous. More work came his way. An **art dealer** named Hendrick was looking for artists to paint portraits. Hendrick lived in Amsterdam. Amsterdam was a seaport and the biggest port in Europe. Ships docked in the harbor and unloaded sugar, cinnamon, or silk to sell in Holland. People grew rich trading and selling. These wealthy people wanted their pictures painted. They'd frame them and enjoy them for years to come. Hendrick invited Rembrandt to paint portraits for him.

MIXING PAINT

Like most painters at the time, Rembrandt made his own paint. He started with chalk, coal, or colored glass. He ground it up into powder on a large, flat stone called a **grindstone**. *The colored powder he made was called* **pigment**. *Next, Rembrandt mixed the powder with oil to make paint.*

Rembrandt made this etching of the Amstel River in Amsterdam.

Rembrandt moved to Amsterdam and started working for Hendrick. Rembrandt's paintings were dark, like other paintings were at the time. But they showed people's feelings better than other painters' works. Rembrandt used black and white paint to outline the person. Then he filled in the outline with color. Rembrandt stroked a little pink onto a woman's cheeks. If she was old, he might paint on a crinkled smile. You could see a rich woman's jewels glitter, even on canvas.

Rembrandt finally finished the two paintings about Jesus. Everyone loved them, including the prince. The prince asked Rembrandt to paint a picture of his wife, Amalia. Rembrandt painted delicate and beautiful lace on Amalia's dress. With the hairs of his paintbrush, Rembrandt painted a string of white pearls. Amalia's pearls glowed from the canvas as if real.

Rembrandt was a big success in Amsterdam. Hendrick introduced him to his niece, Saskia. Rembrandt fell in love with Saskia, and the couple married in 1634. Rembrandt liked painting Saskia. One day, he dressed up in a red velvet robe. He wore a black hat with long white feathers. He painted himself with Saskia sitting on his knee.

The portrait of Amalia is very detailed.

Rembrandt painted Saskia many times. Sometimes she dressed as characters from stories, legends, or the Bible.

Many Dutch people wore black clothes and big, white, round collars. But Rembrandt liked to dress up with Saskia in more colorful clothing. One time, he painted himself dressed up with a large poodle.

Rembrandt earned a lot of money painting and went on a shopping spree. He bought paintings, shells, a leopard skin from Africa, and a small cannon. He bought a large house in the center of Amsterdam. He filled every nook in every room. The house became his gallery and workshop.

Rembrandt taught young apprentices how to paint in his workshop. He had 100 talented pupils during his life. He taught them so well that it was hard to tell which paintings were his students' and which were his! Sometimes a young artist began a painting and Rembrandt

Rembrandt painted many portraits of wealthy people. This painting of a Polish nobleman shows Rembrandt's interest in detailed clothing.

finished it. Rembrandt also signed it. Then he sold the picture as his own because he could get a higher price. Or, if one of his paintings didn't sell, his apprentices changed it and then looked for a buyer again.

You can still see Rembrandt's house in Amsterdam. His old home and workshop is now a museum.

CHAPTER 4

The Night Watch

In 1642, a group of men asked Rembrandt to paint them. They were soldiers who guarded the town. The painting became known as *The Night Watch*. *The Night Watch* is one of the most famous paintings of all time.

    The Night Watch is a painting of a group of soldiers. The captain of the men is wearing a red sash and reaching out his hand. Next to him is a lieutenant carrying a spear. You can almost feel the bumpy gold trim on his coat. The captain and lieutenant look as though they are moving. Having action in paintings was unusual at the time.

    Rembrandt broke another rule. Artists then usually painted everyone the same size. In *The Night Watch*, Rembrandt didn't. The captain and lieutenant look bigger than other soldiers in the painting. Rembrandt used lighter paint on a few people as well. That made them stand out.

    Rembrandt added a woman to the painting, even

THE ARTIST'S SON

Rembrandt made a beautiful portrait of his son, Titus, in 1657. It's now called Titus, The Artist's Son *or* Titus in a Red Hat. *Rembrandt taught his only son how to draw and paint. Titus did not become a great painter like his father did. But with his long, curly-brown hair, he looked like Rembrandt did as a young man.*

though she didn't pose with the men. The woman is dressed in gold. The light seems to be shining on her. The gold paint draws attention to her. The woman looks like Saskia.

The Night Watch *is huge, but it used to be bigger. In the 1700s, someone trimmed off the original painting's edges.*

In later years, Rembrandt began using a technique called **impasto**. He dabbed thick paint on canvas. It was so heavy that it dripped down like mud. Sometimes it clumped. He didn't smooth it out. Rembrandt's paintings looked rougher. He didn't fill in all the details. Yet if you stand back and look at one of these paintings, it is still beautiful. Rembrandt painted *The Jewish Bride* in 1665. The bride touches the groom's hand. The red and gold paint brings a feeling of warmth and love.

In 1668, a serious disease spread through Amsterdam. It was the plague, and many people died. Rembrandt's son Titus caught the plague and died. Rembrandt was certainly heartbroken. He painted a picture of himself looking sadder

This painting is often called The Jewish Bride, *although no one now knows whom it actually shows.*

than ever before. His curly hair had turned white with age. There were wrinkles on his forehead and lines under his eyes. He looked old and tired.

Rembrandt began another painting around that time. It was called *Self-Portrait (as Zeuxis)*, and it was a very dark painting. Rembrandt seems to be laughing, but no one can be sure why. Rembrandt turned 63 in July 1669 and died three months later.

In this painting, some people think Rembrandt was showing himself as an ancient Greek painter named Zeuxis. In legends, Zeuxis laughed himself to death.

Today, Rembrandt's paintings are worth millions of dollars. They are so valuable that thieves steal them from museums. One painting was stolen four times, but the art gallery in London, England, always got it back. It's called the "Takeaway Rembrandt" because it's been stolen so often.

During his life, Rembrandt painted 40 to 50 self-portraits. He also made about 32 etchings of himself. The portraits are like a photo album of his life.

Rembrandt's paintings are masterpieces. He is one of the best painters in history because he didn't paint only what a person looked like on the outside. He also captured the person's spirit and personality inside. His brush showed a little girl's sweetness or a rich man's pride. Rembrandt was also a good teacher to many young artists. He taught talented students how to paint with feeling like he did.

REAL OR FAKE?

Museums sometimes discover that paintings hanging on their walls are not really Rembrandts. Others were only partially painted by the artist. Some are even fakes made by artists who imitated Rembrandt. In 1969, the Dutch government set up the Rembrandt Research Project. Scholars looked at every painting signed by Rembrandt. X-rays helped the experts examine the paint, brushstrokes, and Rembrandt's signature. Sometimes the experts still couldn't tell for sure. Art experts believe that there are between 290 and 320 real Rembrandts in the world.

Rembrandt's portrait of Jacob III de Gheyn, also called the "Takeaway Rembrandt," shows the artist's expression and style.

Glossary

apprentice (uh-PREN-tis) An apprentice is a person who learns a skill by working for an expert. Rembrandt begged his parents to let him become an apprentice to a local painter.

art dealer (ART DEAL-ur) An art dealer buys and sells paintings. An art dealer named Hendrick sold many of Rembrandt's portraits.

canvas (KAN-vuhs) A canvas is a heavy cloth on which a painting is made. Rembrandt made many paintings on canvas.

etchings (ECH-ings) Etchings are pictures or prints that are made from an engraved plate. Many of Rembrandt's first self-portraits were etchings.

grindstone (GRIND-stone) A grindstone is a stone that an artist used to make pigment. Rembrandt ground chalk on his grindstone to make white pigment, and then mixed the pigment with oil to make paint.

impasto (im-PAHS-toe) Impasto is a technique in which painters use thick paint and don't try to smooth it out. As he got older, Rembrandt began experimenting with impasto.

masterpiece (MAS-tur-peese) A masterpiece is an artwork of great excellence. Some people think that *The Night Watch* is Rembrandt's greatest masterpiece.

pigment (PIG-muhnt) Pigment is a substance that gives color to paint. Rembrandt made black pigment by grinding up charcoal into powder.

self-portraits (self POR-trits) Self-portraits are paintings or drawings people create of themselves. Rembrandt painted self-portraits throughout his lifetime.

studio (STOO-dee-oh) A studio is a room or building in which an artist works. Rembrandt opened his first studio in Leiden.

trade (TRADE) A trade is a job or craft, especially one that requires working with one's hands or machines. Back in the 1600s, teenagers would drop out of school and learn a trade.

To Learn More

BOOKS

Blaisdell, Molly. *Rembrandt and the Boy Who Drew Dogs: A Story about Rembrandt van Rijn.* New York: Barrons Educational Series, 2008.

Comora, Madeleine. *Rembrandt and Titus: Artist and Son.* Golden, CO: Fulcrum, 2005.

Roberts, Russell. *Rembrandt.* Hockessin, DE: Mitchell Lane, 2009.

WEB SITES

Visit our Web site for links about Rembrandt:
childsworld.com/links

Note to Parents, Teachers, and Librarians:
We routinely verify our Web links to make sure they are safe and active sites. So encourage your readers to check them out!

Index

Amalia, 12
Amsterdam, 6–7, 11, 12, 14, 15, 18
art dealer, 11

etchings, 4, 20

fakes, 20

Hendrick, 11–12
Huygens, Constantijn, 9, 10

impasto, 18

Jewish Bride, The, 18

Lastman, Pieter, 7–8
Leiden, 6, 7, 9

mixing paint, 11

Night Watch, The, 16

portraits, 11, 12, 16

Rembrandt
  apprenticeship, 6–7
  childhood, 6
  death, 19
  education, 6
  full name, 7
  painting for the prince, 9, 10, 12
  son, 16, 18
  teaching, 14–15
Rembrandt Research Project, 20

Saskia, 12, 14, 17
Self-Portrait (as Zeuxis), 19
self-portraits, 5, 19, 20

"Takeaway Rembrandt," 20
Titus, The Artist's Son, 16
Tobit and Anna with the Kid, 8

Withdrawn